SAVING PLANET EARTH

NEW
DIRECTIONS

Rosalind Kerven

Franklin Watts

London   New York   Sydney   Toronto

CONTENTS

Acknowledgments

The author would like to thank the following for their help: Ark; Friends of the Earth; The Gaia Foundation; Greenpeace; Survival International; Watch; World Wide Fund for Nature.

©1992 Franklin Watts

Franklin Watts
96 Leonard Street
London EC2A 4RH

Franklin Watts
14 Mars Road
Lane Cove
NSW 2066

Series devised by
Rosalind Kerven

Editor
Ruth Taylor

Picture researcher
Sarah Moule

Designed by
Geoff Francis

UK ISBN:0 7496 0824 2
10 9 8 7 6 5 4 3 2 1
Printed in Belgium

A CIP catalogue record for this book is available from the British Library.

Changing Times

Scientists believe that Planet Earth is about 4,500 million years old, and that it has supported life for about 3,000 million years. Yet in the last 200 years, human beings have been polluting and damaging the planet so severely that now the very future of life on Earth may be in danger. How have we achieved such a terrible thing in so short a time?

The story opens with the Industrial Revolution, which began in Britain around 1740. Most of the things which shape our modern way of life have been discovered or invented since then - for example, cars, cameras, electricity, plastic, television and radio, household gadgets and agricultural chemicals. This was also the time when the first large factories opened. Many people moved from their farms and home workshops in the countryside, and went to the big towns and cities to work in them. With the help of new types of machine, the factories began to produce goods such as food, clothes and tools in large quantities, and much more cheaply than before.

Today, in the **rich countries** of Europe, North America, Australia, New Zealand and parts of Asia such as Japan, Hong Kong and Singapore, most people take it for granted that they will be able continuously to buy a wide variety of these factory-made goods.

This Hong Kong shopping centre symbolises a way of life based on the desire to buy as many material goods as possible.

A power station discharges huge clouds of pollution into the air in Moscow, Russia.

The Quest for Economic Growth

When a country's factories make plenty of goods which they then sell at home and abroad, they bring in a lot of money. Some of this money goes to the people themselves, who spend it on more goods. The rest goes in taxes to the government, which may use it to pay for things like roads, hospitals, schools, water pipes and electric power stations. Each of these ways of spending raises people's **standard of living** by making their lives more comfortable. It also encourages factories to produce still more of the goods which are wanted by people and governments with money to spend.

There is thus a continual cycle of making and selling more and more - to earn more money - so that living standards will rise again - and people will want to buy even more goods - and so on. This is known as **economic growth**.

Virtually every government in the world - ranging from the free marketeers of the USA to the authoritarian Communists of China - aims to increase its country's rate of economic growth.

Of course, this has brought numerous vast improvements to people's lives in the rich world: we own countless useful things that people would never have dreamed of 300 years ago. But at the same time it has caused serious damage to the environment.

The "Impossible Party"

Factories need large amounts of **raw materials** such as metal, wood and oil to manufacture their goods. Their machines work by electricity, which at present is usually produced by burning coal, oil, gas or nuclear fuel. Distributing the finished goods uses a lot of petrol.

All these raw materials are Earth's **resources**. Some, such as oil, coal, metals and other minerals, exist only in limited amounts and will eventually run out. Others, such as trees for timber, could possibly last for ever if they were replaced as they were used; but generally this has not happened. Very many of the world's resources are being rapidly used up.

Moreover, the factories which turn raw materials into goods discharge huge amounts of waste into the air, water and land, including poisonous chemicals. As people get richer, more drive cars which add petrol fumes to the general pollution. And vast amounts of rubbish are piling up as goods are thrown away to be replaced by new ones.

Recently, some observers have described this way of life as an "Impossible Party". It is impossible, they say, because it cannot last for ever. Eventually, one resource after another will come to an end. And eventually we will be overwhelmed by rubbish and pollution.

England does not have much unspoiled countryside left. What remains is constantly under pressure from new industrial developments such as this chalk quarry, operated by a cement company.

Too Many People?

In 1990 the world population was estimated to be 5,500 million. It is increasing by about 1 million people every four days. By 2020 there may be 8,500 million people.

Already there is not enough food for everyone. To produce more, ancient forests and wilderness areas are cleared and turned into farmland, causing the people and wild creatures that lived there to lose their homes. The land is sprayed with chemical fertilisers, weed killers and pesticides in an attempt to grow more and better crops. These chemicals sometimes poison the food and water supply.

Only 2 per cent of the world population live in the USA, but their standard of living is so high that currently they are using up about 25 per cent of Earth's resources. If everyone in the world could use as much, many of the things we take for granted would run out completely in a very short time.

The Birth of a New Movement

In 1962 an American biologist, Rachel Carson, published a book called *Silent Spring*. This described the alarming ways in which our present way of life is poisoning the natural environment. It was the first of many warnings in which eminent scientists and others began to urge people - and particularly governments - to change their ways before Planet Earth is damaged beyond repair. The **environmental movement** had been born.

For some years, environmentalists were regarded as cranks and killjoys. But more recently, a number of world events have made the public increasingly mindful of their ideas. Industrial accidents have caused horrifying pollution over wide areas. Probably the most alarming of these was the explosion at the Chernobyl nuclear power station in the USSR in 1986, which carried dangerous radioactivity right across the world. At the same time, strong scientific evidence has shown that gases discharged by industry, power stations and vehicles are changing the global climate, damaging the atmosphere and creating **acid rain** which kills trees and life in lakes and rivers. There are constant news reports about the destruction of the world's last great natural habitats and the extinction of many wild plants and animals.

Turning of the Tide

By the late 1980s the environmental movement - now more commonly known as the **Green movement** - had become a respectable and important part of everyday life. Numerous national leaders have declared their concern for Green issues. Surveys show that the majority of ordinary people, in rich countries at least, have begun to worry about what is happening.

It is becoming generally accepted that the way we live must change if the human race - and indeed the planet itself - is to have a future.

The most radical Green thinkers say that the quest for everlasting economic growth will simply have to stop. At present, this suggestion is not regarded as realistic or acceptable by any government.

However, politicians and industrialists are now discussing the idea of **sustainable growth**. This means continuing to make most of the goods that we are used to - but producing them much more carefully, so that resources are preserved and recycled, and the environment is not harmed in the process or when the goods are thrown away. They are also starting to consider ways of repairing the extensive damage that has already been done.

This book explores some of the progress that has been made so far. Hopefully the tide really is turning, as people all over the world take the first small but significant steps towards saving Planet Earth.

If Planet Earth is really to be saved from environmental disaster, it is vital to change the way that people think about it.

Many problems have been caused by the idea that we humans are in some way "in charge" of the world, and have the right to use and change it however we want. In contrast, Greens point out that human beings are just one of countless living species. Instead of having rights to use (or mis-use) the planet, we have a shared *responsibility* to *look after it*. We should stop trying to twist nature to serve human purposes; instead we should learn to live in balance with natural rhythms and processes.

In the past, scientists and other experts have usually treated each problem they deal with separately. Greens point out that nothing in the world exists in isolation. Therefore, problems cannot be solved, or crises overcome, without taking a **holistic** approach.

For example, if a particular animal species is in danger of extinction, the traditional approach might be to breed it in zoos and then return it to the wild. But even then it might not survive if, say, the forests where it lives are disappearing.

The Green approach would make a priority of safeguarding the forest habitat. This in turn would mean understanding why people were cutting the forest down. It might be because they needed more land to grow food; which, in turn, could be because the local human population was growing too fast to feed itself, and also because existing farm land was being used inefficiently to raise cattle rather than to grow plant foods which are much more highly productive. So, saving a single endangered species becomes an extremely complicated process that would also need to slow down population growth and change farming methods in order to work. Both of these factors would also help the environment in other ways. Thus everything - for good as well as for bad - is inter-related.

Greens question some of people's most basic values. They say that conservation is more important than economic growth. They challenge the usual idea that wealth lies in money and material goods. Instead they say that no society can be considered rich unless it has a guaranteed supply of clean air and water, and fertile, unpolluted land - the things that are basic to survival, yet becoming increasingly rare.

The current way of thinking is very much concerned with living for today. The Green view is to give much more thought to the future, to consider how our children and grandchildren will manage when most of Earth's natural resources are used up and the whole environment is tainted with poisons. Everything people do to the Earth today will have a consequence in years to come.

Greens emphasise the need for diverse groups of people and countries to forget their differences and work together. Planet Earth is our only home and we are all facing the same crisis. *Think globally - act locally* has become an important slogan. It neatly sums up the idea that environmental problems have enmeshed the whole planet, and that to solve them depends on people everywhere making major changes in their own lives.

Kayapo tribespeople in Brazil wander along a new road which has turned their forest home into a wasteland. Repairing the damage caused by this kind of massive devastation requires a holistic approach. If governments are to support schemes to preserve rainforests and their peoples, they must also allow room to increase food production for the fast-growing general population; as well as for industrial expansion to raise the national standard of living.

6

SAVING NATURE

THE THREAT TO NATURE

Everywhere "nature" seems to be disappearing. Most of us in the developed world live in towns where plants and wild creatures are neatly fenced off into gardens and parks. We have little to do with nature in our daily lives. The things we use are generally artificial, made in factories. Even food tends to come in packages, with few reminders that it is produced from living plants and animals. The changing seasons have little effect on us, since we are shielded from the weather in buildings with central heating and air conditioning, and we travel between them in cars and buses.

In the countryside the majority of farmers have given up working alongside nature and instead seem to be constantly fighting against it, using an array of machines and chemicals to raise crops and animals. Many beautiful natural areas are regarded as "wasted" unless they are developed as housing or industrial estates, tourist attractions or out-of-town shopping centres; or have roads built across them to provide closer links between cities.

Increasingly, human beings try to dominate, control and distort what is left of the natural world. Particularly disturbing are new developments in genetic engineering, by which scientists can actually change the basic characteristics of certain living things.

No other species has the power to stop this kind of human activity. It is not surprising that so much of the natural world has been destroyed, or changed beyond recognition.

The Whole Earth is Alive

If the natural world is to survive, people must change their whole attitude towards it. Many scientists are now seriously thinking about the **Gaia Theory**, which was invented by research chemist James Lovelock. This suggests that the planet Earth itself is "alive". Plants and animals, even the elements and the weather are inseparable parts of it, just as our hands are parts of our bodies. All aspects of life on Earth are linked up and interdependent.

For this living Earth to stay healthy, all its parts must be properly looked after. If people damage any part too badly, the whole planet and all its inhabitants may die. Alternatively, human beings may exterminate themselves, allowing the planet to continue life more healthily without them.

Deep Ecology

Deep ecologists have thrown up further challenging ideas. They believe that all species are equally as important as humans and should have the same rights. People should live in harmony with nature and respect it, instead of trying to control and change it. They should take good care of natural resources and only use things that they really need.

God is Green

Some religions such as Hinduism and Buddhism, as well as the religions of tribal peoples (see page 24), have always taught that people should care for other creatures. In contrast, many Christians, Muslims and Jews used to believe that God created humans to be superior and that they therefore had an unlimited right to use and exploit the natural world. Recently, however, Green thinkers from each of these religions have begun to argue that God gave people a special responsibility to look after creation – not the right to destroy it. They are persuading other believers that saving the environment should be part of their religious duty.

People of different religions marched on a pilgrimage to Canterbury Cathedral in Britain, to show their commitment to the environment.

Hugging the Trees

In India thousands of people – particularly women and children – have shown their determination to protect nature by taking part in the **Chipko movement**. In 1973 timber merchants wanted to cut down a large area of public forest. When the government failed to stop them, outraged local villagers joined together to literally "hug the trees", refusing to move until the loggers finally gave up and went away. Other villagers throughout northern India followed their example, and have also planted new woods, making it possible for wild birds and animals to return to their former homes.

Indian villagers "hug the trees".

SAVING NATURE

Joining Up

Growing numbers of people worldwide belong to environmental organisations. In Britain alone, different charities such as Friends of the Earth, the Royal Society for the Protection of Birds and local nature conservation trusts together have about 4 million members. Some of these regularly flood government ministers and other influential people with letters protesting about activities which are harmful to wild creatures and their habitats. Others join local groups which campaign, for example, against developers destroying a neighbourhood beauty spot or wildlife sanctuary. Children and young people are especially active: over 30,000 belong to WATCH, an environmental group which organises major wildlife surveys and other practical nature projects.

British children belonging to the environmental club, WATCH, survey the wildlife in their local pond.

Voting Green

In 1983 large numbers of people in (what was then) West Germany voted for a totally new kind of political party: *die Grünen* (the Greens). With 27 members of the *Bundestag* (national parliament), *die Grünen* were powerful enough to persuade their government into action to save German forests which are dying from acid rain caused by industrial pollution. Four years later they had become even more popular and had 42 members of parliament.

Their success inspired voters elsewhere to support parties whose main aim is to protect the environment. In Britain 15 per cent of voters supported the Green Party in elections for the European Parliament in 1989. Green parties are also growing in importance in other parts of Europe, Australia, the USA and Canada.

A postcard produced by die Grünen. (Artist: Bernd Pfarr/Die Grünen)

DIE GRÜNEN

Farmers for Nature

Farmers everywhere have often been blamed for using herbicides, pesticides and other chemicals which poison much wildlife. But some have now returned to **organic farming**, in which all chemicals are banned and farmers fertilise their crops naturally. This gives a chance for wild flowers and insects to flourish again and thus increases the numbers of birds and other animals that feed on them.

A lot of pollution is currently caused by cotton farmers, who depend greatly on insecticides. In the early 1990s, a small group in the USA grew their first crop of organic cotton. They kept geese in their fields to eat some of the pests.

Some British farmers are now officially paid by the government if they preserve or recreate special types of rare natural landscapes and wildlife habitats.

A wide strip along the edge of a cornfield is left untouched to encourage wildlife.

A fox brings a touch of wild nature to a perfectly manicured suburban garden.

Gardening for Wildlife

Even in towns, people are starting to work with nature instead of against it. **Wildlife gardening** has become fashionable, and some gardeners are finding that native wild flowers can make just as beautiful displays as exotic tropical types. Even clumps of stinging nettles are sometimes allowed to stay, because they attract butterflies. Garden ponds often now contain native frogs instead of imported goldfish. Feeding wild birds has always been popular, but some people now put food out to attract urban foxes, badgers and (in North America) raccoons.

11

SAVING VITAL RESOURCES

WE CAN'T LIVE WITHOUT THEM

Air, water and land are all essential to life as we know it; yet human beings are polluting and wasting all three at an alarming rate.

Industrial chemicals which escape into the air are heating the world's climate and changing weather patterns through the **Greenhouse Effect**. They are destroying the **ozone layer** in the atmosphere, which protects Earth from the Sun's dangerous radiation. They also cause acid rain. In some cities such as Athens (Greece) and Bombay (India), pollution from car fumes and industry is bad enough to cause severe illness and breathing difficulties. The water in many rivers is too polluted to drink; the oceans are tainted with dangerous waste; and many countries, including China and the USA, have severe water shortages. Human activity is turning much land that was once fertile and lush into barren deserts.

Earth's other valuable resources are also being carelessly wasted, mainly by people in the rich countries. Trees which took decades to grow are cut down to make disposable paper products; not nearly enough are replanted. Minerals such as oil and coal are rapidly used up, even though they can never be replaced.

Many resources are *literally* wasted. Goods are wrapped in layers of paper and plastic packaging which are immediately thrown away. Machines, which took vast quantities of metal and energy to make, break down and are discarded after only a few years.

The world's rubbish dumps are growing ever bigger. But the stock of resources needed for a healthy, decent life is shrinking fast.

This shanty town on Smokey Mountain in the Philippines has been built in the midst of a vast rubbish dump.

Cleaning Up the World's Air

Governments throughout the world are realising at last that radical new laws are needed to protect Earth's resources.

In the 1980s the first ever global treaties to fight air pollution were signed. Governments across the world agreed to cut down drastically on discharges of the chemicals which are destroying the ozone layer.

A similar international agreement to reduce the pollutants which cause the Greenhouse Effect is also urgently required. Most rich countries, including those in the European Community, are already taking such action. However, the world's worst polluter, the USA, has so far (in 1991) refused to participate.

A scientist in Antarctica studying damage to the atmosphere's protective ozone layer.

In Bologna, Italy, trams help keep the city centre traffic-free.

All Change in the Cities

Nevertheless, many Americans realise that they cannot wait for their national government to lead the way.

Los Angeles is the country's most polluted city. In 1989 local authorities there ordered that factories making goods such as paint would in future have to reduce their use of toxic chemicals. They will place limits on how many cars any single household can own; people will be encouraged to use energy-efficient public transport more; and all vehicles using petrol or diesel will have been banned by 2007, probably by replacing them with alcohol-based fuel. Lawn mowers and barbecues that use petrol will be banned.

Neighbouring Davis, California, has already shown how towns really can clean themselves up. Cars are in the minority there: most people get about by bicycle. Almost everyone tries to save energy and recycle their rubbish. Thousands of trees have been planted, which help to freshen the air.

European cities are also trying to reduce air pollution from traffic fumes. For example, cars are to be banned from parking in a large area of central Paris, France; and Bologna, Italy, has free public transport and restricts the use of cars.

13

Replacing What's Been Lost

Planting new trees in Kenya.

Trees are vital to Planet Earth's health. They affect global weather patterns. They hold together fragile soils which would otherwise be blown away and turn into desert. They provide food and shelter for numerous creatures. They yield wood for fuel, building materials and industry. Yet most of the world's great forests have now been cut down.

Britain is one of the least forested countries in the world: only 10 per cent of it is covered by trees (compared with 67 per cent of Japan). Now there are plans to "green" its towns and cities by planting about twelve new community forests on the edge of big urban areas such as east London and Tyneside. There will also be a large new national forest in England's Midlands; and small areas of woodland will be planted on wasteland such as railway embankments inside the towns themselves.

In Vietnam massive areas of forest were destroyed during its long war which ended in 1975, and in the re-building which followed it. Since 1986 the Vietnamese government has been trying to plant millions of new trees every year. All school children there have to plant their own tree and look after it.

Sometimes individuals achieve more than governments. In Kenya, one woman, Wangari Maathai, started the **Green Belt Movement** which has inspired and helped ordinary people to plant over 10 million trees across the country. Many of these are cared for as they grow, by teams of children.

Environment-Friendly Shopping

Manufacturers have begun to realise that demand is growing for goods that do not damage or waste vital resources.

Sales of washing-up liquid and laundry liquid which claim not to pollute the water supply are booming. All sorts of appliances, from central heating boilers to light bulbs, are advertised as using very little energy or fuel. It has become fashionable to print leaflets and books, and to write letters on paper labelled as **"recycled"**. In Britain a recent survey showed that 40 per cent of shoppers always try to buy **environment-friendly** products.

Green shoppers in Germany have been able to choose goods with official "Blue Angel" labels since 1978. These are a sign that making and using the goods causes very little damage to the environment. The European Community plans to extend this labelling scheme into all 12 of its member states, possibly in 1992. Similar schemes already operate in Canada and Japan.

A combined heat and power station in Finland.

Using Less

There is only one significant way to save fuels such as oil and coal: use less.

In Sweden, Finland and the Netherlands, homes in some towns and cities are centrally heated by the "waste" heat which normally escapes from power stations generating electricity. This **Combined Heat and Power** gets twice as much energy from the same amount of fuel - so only half as much is needed.

Some new homes in Sweden have been designed to keep the warmth in so well that they need only 10 per cent of the normal amount of heating.

Using It Again

Despite voluntary recycling schemes, most boxes, bottles, tubs, tubes and wrappers still end up in rubbish dumps.

In Britain a supermarket chain now actually pays its customers to re-use plastic carrier bags. In 1991 this saved over 50 million new bags - the equivalent of 1 million barrels of oil.

Germany has a new law which should almost bring an end to the "throw-away" habit there. By 1995 80 per cent of all consumer goods packaging will have to be taken back by the manufacturers for recycling.

Volunteers in Britain collect aluminium cans for recycling.

WHAT THE WILDERNESS IS WORTH

A wilderness is a stretch of land where nature controls itself and where plants and animals live largely undisturbed by human activity. Examples are the world's last great forests, the tundras of the Arctic and the icy wastes of Antarctica.

Wildernesses show how all non-human life on Earth might be if people did not alter and manipulate it. They contain countless species, many as yet unknown to science. Some of these could be very useful to people in the future, as new food crops, medicines or industrial materials. But apart from such usefulness, many people now feel that wildernesses and their inhabitants have an intrinsic right to exist and be protected.

There is probably no wilderness on Earth totally untouched by humans. Helicopters roar over the vast rainforests of the Amazon. Traces of poisonous chemicals have been found in the sea creatures of Antarctica. Air pollution drifts across the whole planet.

All wildernesses are fighting for survival. The rainforests are being rapidly cut down. Governments and international mining companies are eager to extract the wildernesses' rich underground stores of oil and other minerals.

In the past, wildernesses were regarded as wild, dangerous places that ought to be tamed and exploited. Only now, with hardly any left, are ideas about them starting to change towards conservation.

The world's first National Park: Yellowstone, USA.

Protecting Special Places

Most countries now contain **National Parks** and similar protected areas. These are supposed to safeguard unspoiled places and their wildlife against damaging human activity.

The world's first National Park, Yellowstone in the USA, dates from 1872. There are now about 5,000 of them covering approximately 3 per cent of the Earth's land surface; but many conservationists feel that there should be at least three times as many.

About 90 outstandingly important areas are **World Heritage Sites** which receive extra international protection.

A World Heritage Site: The Great Barrier Reef, Australia.

Many of the countries which still contain large wilderness areas are very poor. They have borrowed money from the richer countries to try to feed their hungry people, but cannot afford to pay it back.

In recent years various environmental organisations have offered to pay back some of this money; in return, the country which owes it promises to conserve an area of its wilderness. This is known as "swapping debts for nature". The World Wide Fund for Nature (WWF) has operated such schemes successfully in countries such as Ecuador, the Philippines and Madagascar.

They include the Great Barrier Reef in Australia and the British island of St Kilda.

Unfortunately, National Parks do not always work very well. Some are over-run by tourists - for example, in Africa, where holidays on game reserves are increasingly popular. If minerals are discovered in National Parks, governments may decide that the money to be earned from allowing mining there is worth more to them than conserving a special place. Moreover, in some Parks, local people feel they are "fenced out" of their own land, and resent being told how to look after it by foreign conservationists.

In Africa the National Parks and their wild inhabitants are under constant pressure from tourists.

The Rainforests

Every year an area of tropical rainforest bigger than the United Kingdom (30 million hectares) is lost. Some forests are cut down for their exotic timber which is sold to countries such as Britain and Japan. Others are turned into ranches to rear cattle for beef, or small farms to feed the rapidly growing populations of desperately poor local people. And others are cleared to build roads, dams or mines.

Governments that have rainforests need to find ways in which the forests can earn money without being damaged or destroyed.

Some countries selling tropical wood products have begun to practise sustainable timber production, which aims to plant a new tree for each one cut down. However, it takes decades for the new trees to grow, and before they do so, gaps in the forest may harm the fragile habitat over a much larger area. A recent British survey found that many companies are dishonest in claiming to sell only "sustainable" rainforest wood. Because of these problems, some customers now refuse to buy tropical timber of any kind.

The best hope for the future is to harvest the type of natural forest goods which re-grow every year.

These include latex-sap from rubber trees (made into tyres and other rubber products); rattan (creeping vines used for ropes, furniture and baskets);nuts and fruits. But even this activity must be controlled: wild rattan is already becoming rare.

Some industrial companies which have harmed rainforests in the past are now trying to "green" their operations. In the Amazon a company mining aluminium ore now replants the patches of forest it destroys and is making efforts to conserve the surrounding areas.

Tapping rubber trees in Brazil - an activity which does not harm the rainforest.

Selling rainforest fruits at a local market in Zaire.

The Last Great Wilderness

Antarctica is recognised as Earth's only real remaining wilderness. Although almost entirely covered by ice up to 3 kilometres thick, it is rich in wildlife including penguins and other birds, whales, seals and fish. It has no native human population. However, many countries have sent scientists to study Antarctica and the areas where they have lived are littered with things they have left behind.

Antarctica. Many Greens would like to see it declared a "World Park".

Thirty-nine countries belong to the Antarctic Treaty. Since 1961 this has set aside the continent for peaceful purposes only and banned nuclear testing and waste disposal there. Some members support the idea of declaring Antarctica a "World Park", totally protected from human activity for all time.

However, other countries have been eager to obtain the rich supplies of minerals, including coal, iron and uranium, which are believed to lie under the ice. Environmentalists who have campaigned strongly against this regarded it as a great victory when all the Treaty members agreed to ban any mining in Antarctica for 50 years from 1991. This ban may eventually become permanent if the USA can be persuaded to agree.

Friends of the Bog

Parts of Britain are covered by wild peat-bog, which provides an important home to rare species of plants, insects and birds.

Some has temporarily disappeared under timber plantation. Large-scale peat extraction is destroying much of what remains - even areas which are supposed to be protected as **Sites of Special Scientific Interest**. Peat is widely used by professional horticulturalists and amateur gardeners. Ninety-six per cent of British raised peat-bog has been lost in 140 years.

Many people have stopped buying peat for their gardens, and some shops have stopped selling it. Gardening supply companies are developing new environment-friendly alternatives to peat. If most people stop buying it, large-scale peat extraction will stop and the remaining bogs may be saved. Even such small wilderness areas are important to preserve the full variety of Earth's living species.

A peat-bog in Ireland. For centuries people have cut the peat by hand to burn on their fires. Now areas such as this are threatened by large-scale mechanical extraction.

SAVING OTHER SPECIES

THE VARIETY OF LIFE

Some of Earth's most intelligent creatures, such as these gorillas, are in danger of extinction.

No-one is sure how many different species there are on Planet Earth. So far nearly 1.5 million different plants, animals and micro-organisms are known to science - but the true figure is guessed at between 5 and 30 million.

Scientists estimate that humankind may be driving at least one species a day to extinction. By the year 2050 half of all the species alive now could have disappeared.

The main cause is the destruction of wildlife habitats, such as forests and even old-fashioned hay-meadows. For every plant that dies out, up to 30 kinds of insects and animals that feed on it may also disappear.

The full variety of species is probably very important to the overall health of the planet (see the Gaia Theory, page 8); it is certainly vital to people. Three-quarters of human food comes from just seven plants: wheat, rice, maize, potato, barley, sweet-potato and cassava. If these were ever blighted by disease or pests, mass starvation could be avoided by learning to cultivate some of the 75,000 other plant species which are known to be edible - so long as they are not already extinct. Other endangered plants could yield powerful new types of medicine or industrial materials.

Many well-known species of animals are currently facing possible extinction, including gorillas, elephants, rhinos and tigers. It will probably not make much difference to human welfare if they disappear. But a world containing only people and a few "useful" plants and animals would be a very bleak place indeed.

Seed Banks

About 60 countries have national **seed banks** where they aim to store samples of seeds from every variety of local crop. There are also international seed banks such as the one in the Philippines which contains 60,000 different types of rice; and the Mexican centre which keeps 12,000 types of wheat and maize from 47 countries.

Seeds from these banks may be needed urgently to develop new, extra-hardy varieties of food crops as pollution causes Earth's climate to change (see page 12).

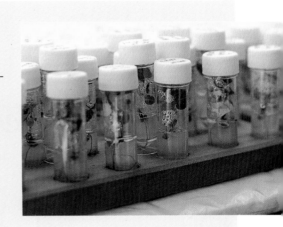

A seed bank at the International Institute for Tropical Agriculture in Nigeria.

Gardeners Show the Way

Storing seeds in banks is expensive and, after some years, seeds may spoil and fail to grow. It is important to keep them alive and usable by growing them as often as possible. This can also be expensive and time-consuming, as to keep them pure, plants may need to be pollinated by hand.

Amateur gardeners play a key part in this work. Seed Savers Exchange in the USA has hundreds of ordinary members who actively grow about 5,000 rare varieties of vegetables and fruits in their gardens, and then swap the seeds. Many of these are unknown to official seed banks. Similar groups exist in a number of European countries including Germany and Britain. In 1991 they launched a "Save Our Seeds" campaign to raise money for seed-saving and also to encourage more people to grow rare varieties.

For a healthy planet it is important to save *all* plants - not just "useful" ones. In Britain private gardeners have set up National Plant Collections, each of which aims to contain all known varieties of a particular ornamental plant, ranging from daisies to beech trees.

One of Britain's National Plant Collections shows off the many different varieties of dahlia flowers.

Worth More Alive Than Dead!

Many species of animal have been hunted nearly to extinction because their skins, horns or tusks are worth large sums of money.

In 1973, 95 countries signed a treaty known as **CITES** (Convention on International Trade in Endangered Species). This was supposed to safeguard rare species such as rhinos and tigers from being killed and sold abroad.

Unfortunately, Green campaigners feel that CITES is not strict enough, and poachers and smugglers often manage to evade its rules. An organisation called **TRAFFIC** acts internationally to catch people who sell rare animal products illegally.

Perhaps the best way to persuade governments to protect endangered animals is to show that they are worth more alive than dead. In Rwanda, official armed guards have totally protected wild gorillas from poachers since 1984. As a result, tourists have flocked to see them, bringing much money into this impoverished African country.

Elefriends

A hundred years ago there were 10 million elephants in Africa; now only about 600,000 are left. They have been killed for their beautiful ivory tusks which are very valuable.

In 1989 a campaign called Elefriends was launched to save them. Its aim is to persuade people everywhere not to buy or use ivory. In this way it will become worthless and there will be no more point in killing elephants.

In the same year, the President of Kenya publicly burned an enormous pile of ivory which his guards had confiscated from elephant poachers. It was a powerful symbol of how governments are starting to accept responsibility for wildlife.

A pile of ivory, confiscated from elephant poachers, being burned in Kenya.

Even Spiders Matter

As Green ideas become more common-place, even big companies are developing a new outlook, and even the smallest species are being protected.

The only colony of great raft spiders in Britain faced extinction. Its marshland home was drying out as the water was being extracted for people to drink.

In 1991 the water company in charge decided to rescue the spiders by pumping specially purified water back into their marshes. It also began searching for a new source of water so as not to disturb the spiders - even though that may prove very expensive.

The Biggest Creatures on Earth

Protesters from Greenpeace blocking a Russian whaling ship.

Whales are the largest animals ever to have existed on Earth. Sperm whales have brains six times larger than a human brain. Yet many species have been hunted nearly to extinction for their meat and other products.

In the 1970s dramatic and dangerous campaigns began, to ban whale hunting. Organisations such as Greenpeace sent tiny boats to get in the way of the big whaling ships. As a result, public opinion world-wide came to support the whales so strongly that in 1982 almost all of the major whaling nations, including the former USSR, agreed to stop.

Japan, Iceland and Norway want to continue whaling. They argue that small numbers can be caught without putting the species in danger. However, it looks as if other countries will refuse to lift the ban. Saving the whales has become a powerful symbol of the Green movement.

The great raft spider, endangered because of human activity, is currently being rescued at great expense by a British water company.

23

SAVING A WAY OF LIFE

200 MILLION TRIBAL PEOPLE

Some of the world's remaining wilderness areas in over 70 countries are still inhabited by small, isolated societies known to outsiders as "tribal" or "native" people. They include the rainforest peoples of Central and South America and South East Asia, the Inuit (Eskimos) of Greenland and Canada, the Saami (Lapps) of Scandinavia and the Pygmies and Bushmen of Africa.

These people usually live very close to nature and the land, without machines and with relatively few material goods. They do not "go to work" or use money. They obtain food by hunting, fishing, gathering wild plants, herding animals or simple farming. Other things that they need, such as houses, clothes and tools, they mostly make themselves.

Many of the homelands of such tribal societies have now been taken over by neighbouring peoples and their national governments, who have totally different values. Traditional hunting, herding and gathering grounds have been transformed by major roads, mines, ranches, plantations and cities.

Tribal people themselves have been dismissed as "primitive", because they have no use for science or technology as we understand it.

Huge numbers have died: some have been murdered, others have wasted away from alien diseases, or because they could not cope with the shock of modern society. Many of those who remain have been rounded up into small reservations where the land is poor. They have been humiliated and brainwashed in an attempt to force them to share the values of the developed world.

Kayapo women in Brazil. Most tribal peoples understand how to cultivate small tracts of land without harming the structure of the rainforest.

24

A Pygmy family at home in Uganda.

Do They Know Something We Don't Know?

An Inuit man hunting seal in Greenland. Traditional tribal hunters kill only what they personally need, and use almost the entire animal.

Green thinkers admire how tribal people live in harmony with their environment, taking care not to exhaust the land or use up the natural resources upon which they depend. They are urging the rest of the world to save tribal peoples' lives - but also to save their cultures and ways of life, which represent a great store of human knowledge and wisdom about the natural world.

Tribal people are very knowledge-able about the plants and wild creatures that share their lands, including countless different species of which our scientists have never heard.

For example, the Lacondan Maya people of Mexico grow more than 70 different plants as food crops. About three-quarters of plant-based drugs used by doctors in the developed world are based on medicinal herbs used by tribal people.

Rainforest tribes such as the Tsembaga of New Guinea and the Kayapo of Brazil understand how to cultivate the forest without harming it. They practise **shifting agriculture** - chopping and burning down small areas where they grow a rich variety of food crops for a few years. Then they move on, leaving the land untouched for about twenty years, so that it has a chance to become fertile again, and the forest can re-grow. This is in strong contrast to modern farming methods which permanently remove most of the natural vegetation and exhaust the soil by growing the same crops intensively year after year.

Hunting tribes such as the Inuit of the Arctic and the Pygmies of Central Africa kill only what they need to eat. Inedible parts are used for tools and clothes. Almost nothing is wasted, in the hope of ensuring an abundant supply for the future. This seems wiser than developed peoples' recent practice of hunting some animals to extinction (see page 20).

SAVING A WAY OF LIFE

Learning to Respect the Spirits

In Australia a powerful company wanted to mine gold from the Kakadu National Park. This is the homeland of the Jawoyn aborigine people. Much of the landscape is very important to their religion: they believe that a sacred ancestral spirit lives in the rocks. If these were destroyed by miners, they would feel as devastated as Christians whose churches were smashed up.

In the past, the Australian government has ignored such aboriginal concerns. But in 1991 the Prime Minister made history by forbidding mining on these sacred sites.

An aborigine man in the Kakadu National Park, Australia.

Somewhere Safe to Live

A Kuna woman in Panama.

In Central and South America many tribal peoples fear invasion by settlers from the continent's overflowing cities. Newcomers usually destroy the forests, and bring pollution, dangerous diseases and alien values and life-styles.

The Kuna of Panama have controlled their own lands for 50 years. In the 1970s they set up a project to ensure that outsiders help them instead of exploiting them. Tourists and scientists must pay to visit their land, and scientists must always be accompanied by a Kuna and leave them a record of their work.

In Venezuela the government declared a huge area of rainforest a "biosphere reserve" in 1991. The Yanomami and Yekuana people who live there will be protected from outside intruders or developers, encouraged to maintain their traditional life-styles and given special medical help. They will be actively involved in looking after the reserve, which contains a variety of unique, unspoiled landscapes including river, swamps, mountains and different types of forest. In Colombia the government has also recently handed over a large area of forest land to local tribes.

In Brazil the Xavante forced outside loggers and ranchers to leave their land in 1982. They have burned the sawmills, planted new trees and left the exhausted soil to recover naturally. Eventually they hope that enough wild animals may return for them to become traditional-style hunters again.

for tribal peoples

Working Together to Save the Planet

Green campaigners and tribal people are increasingly working together to preserve Earth's remaining wild places and natural resources, and also to persuade the rest of the world to live in harmony with the natural environment.

In Botswana the government planned to extract water for agriculture, mines and diamond mining from the Okavango Delta, a unique swampland, rich in wildlife. International environmentalists campaigned against the plan but it was a protest meeting by 500 local tribespeople (who use the swampland for fishing and gathering wild plants) which, in 1991, finally persuaded the government to change its mind.

The government of Brazil planned to build a series of hydro-electric dams which would flood vast areas of rainforest around the Xingu river. In 1989 about a thousand people from

various local tribes came together for a mass protest meeting. Their impassioned speeches inspired public opinion around the world and helped persuade the World Bank not to pay for the scheme, which was therefore cancelled.

In Irian Jaya, Indonesia, an international company wanted to replace a large stretch of rainforest with plantations of alien eucalyptus trees, which would be pulped to make disposable tissues and toilet paper for the rich world. Environmentalists from many countries supported the 15,000 local Auyu tribespeople who opposed this, and persuaded the paper company to withdraw.

Kayapo Indians with land which would have been flooded by dams on the Xingu river.

Two men from the Kelabit and Penan tribes of Sarawak, Malaysia, speak to British journalists about the destruction of their local rainforests.

Always on Guard

Many people in the developed world now sympathise strongly with tribal peoples. Survival International is a charity which works on their behalf. It emphasises listening to what such people want, not imposing outside ideas on them. It has 12,000 members in over 60 countries.

27

The environment is beginning to dominate thinking across the world. People at all levels want to do something positive to try to change things, and the Green movement is gathering momentum.

Yet the encouraging developments you have just read about are mere drops in the ocean. We are still wasting resources, destroying natural habitats and pumping out pollution at ever-increasing rates. Almost every week it seems that some new environmental outrage hits the headlines.

The most radical campaigners - often known as "Dark Greens" - ask how long we can delay while governments and industrialists argue over exactly what needs to be done and how to do it. They are quite sure that very soon life will have to change fundamentally. They say we will have to stop trying to get richer all the time and instead concentrate on clearing up the mess we have made of the planet. We will no longer be able to take anything for granted: for example, we may have to stop using throw-away paper and plastic products; and give up travelling by car or aeroplane except for essential journeys. Not surprisingly, most people find these ideas disturbing, and at present they are not widely accepted.

Other campaigners - the "Light Greens" - are more optimistic about the small steps which have already been taken. They feel that if we continue to move

People of all ages at a Green demonstration in Hungary. The Green movement has only just begun in Eastern Europe, much of which has suffered some of the worst industrial pollution in the world.

further in the same direction, Planet Earth may yet be saved without destroying our current way of life.

Most Greens are totally against the idea of forcing through the changes that are needed by any kind of violent revolution. Instead they urge co-operation and harmony in all spheres. Indeed, many of the improvements that have already happened are the result of ordinary people taking action for themselves.

Ailton Krenak, a leader of the rainforest people of Brazil, summed up the spirit of where the Green movement is going with these words:

"There is another way of living on Earth without stopping the rivers, without dragging out its heart, without destroying nature's gardens, which are the forests...

We want to balance the rhythm of things...

We want to show that it is possible for the human race to achieve their adventure ... with nature alive."

GLOSSARY

acid rain Polluted rainfall caused by gases discharged into the air from industry, power stations and vehicles.

Chipko movement A form of mass protest in India, in which villagers prevent outsiders from cutting down their forests by "hugging the trees".

CITES The Convention on International Trade in Endangered Species – intended to stop rare species of animals from being sold abroad.

Combined Heat and Power A system in which the "waste" heat normally discharged from electric power stations is used to heat nearby homes and offices.

Deep ecology A way of seeing the world which believes that all species have the same values and rights as human beings.

economic growth The process in which all countries try to increase their wealth by producing more and more goods.

environment-friendly Used to describe anything which causes no harm to the natural environment.

environmental movement The mixed collection of people and groups throughout the world who are trying to save Earth's natural environment.

Gaia Theory An idea invented by scientist James Lovelock which sees Planet Earth as a single "living" system.

Green Used to describe a person, thing, system or idea that gives priority to protecting life and the natural environment.

Green movement Another name for the environmental movement (see above).

Green Belt Movement A collection of ordinary people throughout Kenya who have planted millions of trees.

Greens People who consider themselves to be part of the environmental movement (see above).

Greenhouse Effect The process by which industrial chemicals discharged into the air are heating up the world climate and changing weather patterns.

holistic A way of looking at a thing or a problem from an overall point of view, rather than splitting it up into separate parts.

National Park A relatively unspoiled natural area which is given special protection by a country's government.

organic farming A system of farming which uses only natural fertilisers and pest control, and from which artificial chemicals are banned.

ozone layer A gas in the atmosphere which protects Earth and its inhabitants from the sun's dangerous radiation.

raw materials Things such as wood or metal from which goods are manufactured.

recycled Used again: for example, a material such as paper or glass, or a product such as a milk bottle, is used again instead of being thrown away.

resources Things essential to life: air, water and land. Also naturally occurring substances such as wood and minerals which can be used to make goods.

rich countries Countries in which almost everyone has the basic necessities of life, and enjoys a good standard of living (see below). Most of the countries of western Europe, the USA, Canada, Australia, New Zealand, Hong Kong, Japan and Singapore.

seed bank A collection of seeds from many different species of plants, which are carefully preserved for the future.

shifting agriculture A system of farming, often practised by tribal peoples, in which a plot is cultivated for a few years and then left to recover naturally while the farmers move on to another plot.

Sites of Special Scientific Interest
Small areas of natural land in Britain containing so many important wild plants and animals that they are supposed to be given extra protection.

standard of living The level of material comfort enjoyed by a person, a group of people or a country.

sustainable growth A type of economic growth (see above) which uses resources (see above) in such a way that there will still be enough left for the long-term future.

TRAFFIC An international organisation which tries to stop people breaking the law by selling rare animal products.

wildlife gardening A way of gardening that attracts wild creatures such as birds, butterflies and squirrels.

World Heritage Sites Outstandingly beautiful or unusual places in various countries which receive extra international protection.

Helpful Organisations

Please contact the following for full details of their publications and price lists.

ARK
498 - 500 Harrow Road, London W9 3QA. Tel: 081-968 6780
Aims "to help people learn more about the environment and lead greener lives". Various booklets, videos and other useful materials, for children and adults.

FRIENDS OF THE EARTH
26 - 28 Underwood Street, London N1 7JQ. Tel: 071-490 1555
"One of the leading environmental pressure groups in the UK ... A positive force for change, not just opposing environmental abuse, but proposing constructive solutions." Many information leaflets suitable for children available from the Education Department. Schools which join SCHOOL FRIENDS receive special packs of educational material and project sheets. Youth membership is available and young people over 14 can join campaigns organised by EARTH ACTION.

FRIENDS OF THE EARTH (Australia)
P.O. Box A474, Sydney South, NSW 2000

Picture Credits:

Cover: Trygve Bølstad/Panos Pictures

Alcan Aluminium Can Recycling 15B; Australian Overseas Information Service 17T; Robert Brook 4, David England 19L, R. Hadley 17B, 22, H. Girardet 7, 24, C. Jones 20, V. Miles 11R, Peter Musgrave 19R/The Environmental Picture Library; Monique Cabral 27L, Brenda Prince 27L/Format; Finnpower 15T; Baker 23L, Midgley 13L, Plowden 18L/Greenpeace; Robert Harding Picture Library 26L; Liba Taylor/Hutchison Library 3B; Northern Territories Tourist Commission 26R; T. Exley/National Council for the Conservation of Plants and Gardens 21B; Trygve Bølstad 14R, J. Hartley 28, Roderick Johnson 9B, Bruce Paton 21T, Nick Robinson 18R, 25L/Panos Pictures; A.K. Rivett 23R; Spectrum 3T; E. Chalke/Survival International 27R; United States Travel and Tourism Administration 16; Victoria Pope/Watch Trust for Environmental Education 10T; Jack Jackson 25R, Ann Wilson 9T/WWF UK; L.W. Wyatt 11L.

30

THE GAIA FOUNDATION

18 Well Walk, Hampstead, London NW3 1LD. Tel: 071-435 5000 Concerned with "people and projects working to protect and revitalise ... the living Earth". Much of their work is concerned with rainforest peoples. Fact sheets and other material available for school children.

GREENPEACE

Canonbury Villas, London N1 2PN. Tel: 071-354 5100/071-359 7396 A campaigning organisation which "stands for a safe and nuclear-free world, fresh air, clean water, the protection of wildlife and their habitats". Nothing specifically for children, but their various fact sheets and reports may be useful for older readers.

GREENPEACE AUSTRALIA

Private Bag 6, P.O. Box Broadway 2007

SURVIVAL INTERNATIONAL

310 Edgware Road, London W2 1DY. Tel: 071-723 5535 "A worldwide movement to support tribal peoples ... and help them protect their lands, environment and way of life." Educational and "action" packs suitable for children of different ages. Special young people's membership provides "Urgent Action Bulletins" and newsletters and encourages participation in letter-writing campaigns. Many other publications, videos, slide shows, etc also available.

WATCH

The Green, Witham Park, Waterside South, Lincoln LN5 7JR Tel: 0522-544400 "A national club for young people who care about wildlife and the environment." Members can take part in national projects and competitions. There are also local WATCH clubs throughout the UK, and special facilities for schools and youth groups. Various publications and project packs.

W.W.F. (U.K.) - WORLD WIDE FUND FOR NATURE

Panda House, Weyside Park, Catteshall Lane, Godalming, Surrey GU7 1XR. Tel: 0483-426444 "The world's largest international nature conservation organisation." Operates a special junior club called GO WILD! Also publishes many fact sheets and other materials including resource packs and "environmental musicals" suitable for performance by school children.

Further Reading

THE GREEN GUIDE TO CHILDREN'S BOOKS published by Books for Keeps, 6 Brightfield Road, Lee, London SE12 8QF (price £6.50), gives details of numerous books for all ages concerned with saving the environment - including fiction and poetry as well as many excellent information books.

BBC WILDLIFE magazine, available monthly from good newsagents, or by subscription from BBC Wildlife, P.O. Box 125, Tonbridge, Kent TN9 1YP, contains regular news of developments, both good and bad, in the global environmental movement, as well as high-quality features on all aspects of the natural world.

INDEX

32

PRINTED IN BELGIUM BY

INTERNATIONAL BOOK PRODUCTION

7·7·98